A PICNIC FOR EVERYONE

FEEDING THE CROWDS

"Give to others, and God will give to you." from Luke 6:38

Written by Juli Foreman and Tricia Clem
Illustrated by Kevin Foreman

Long ago, in a house by a very big lake, a young boy lived with his parents.

His mother and father often talked about a man named Jesus. They told the boy that Jesus made sick people well. Jesus even made a blind man see. Most of all, Jesus loved everyone. "I wish I could see Jesus," the boy said as he went to bed that night.

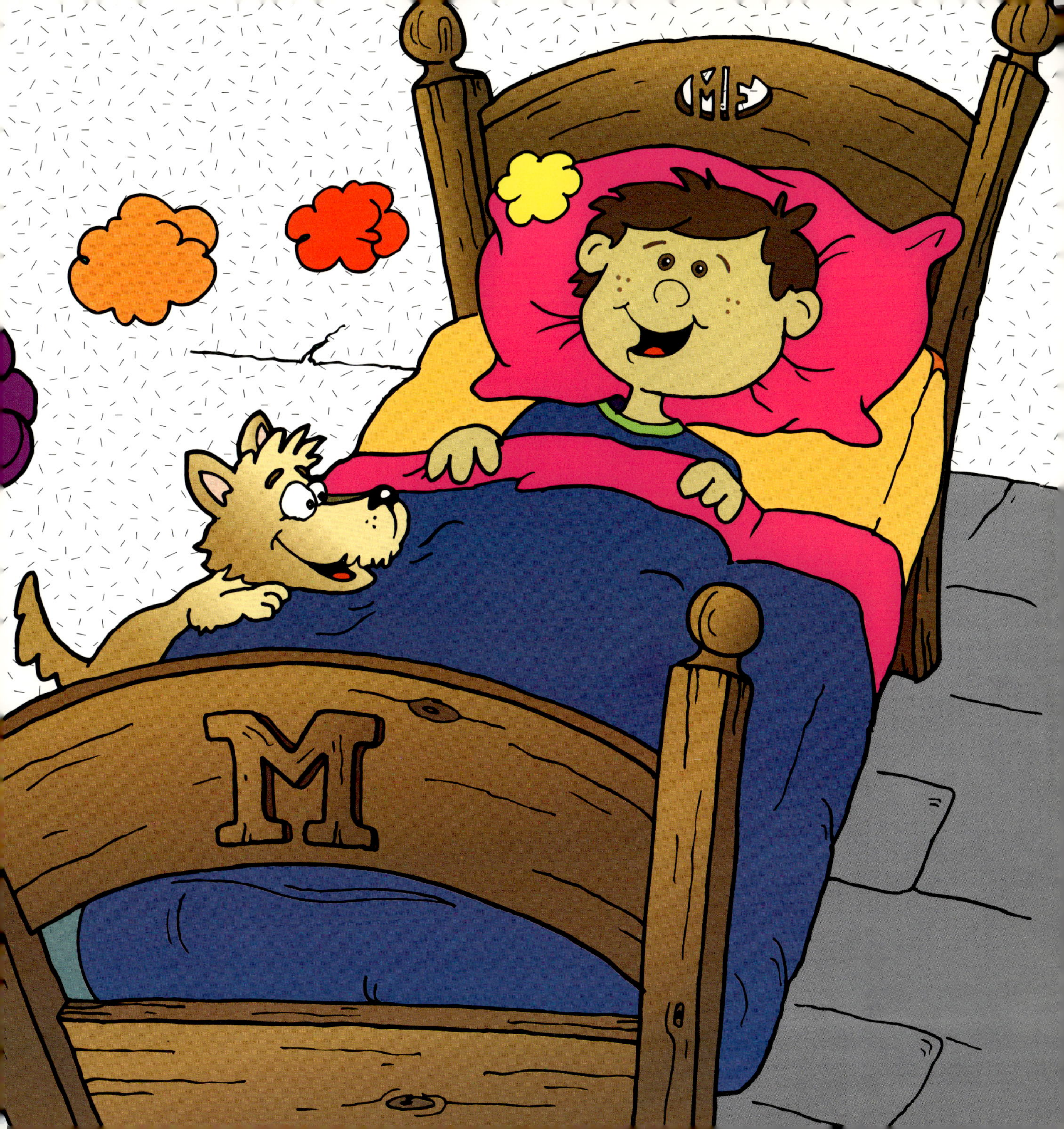
M

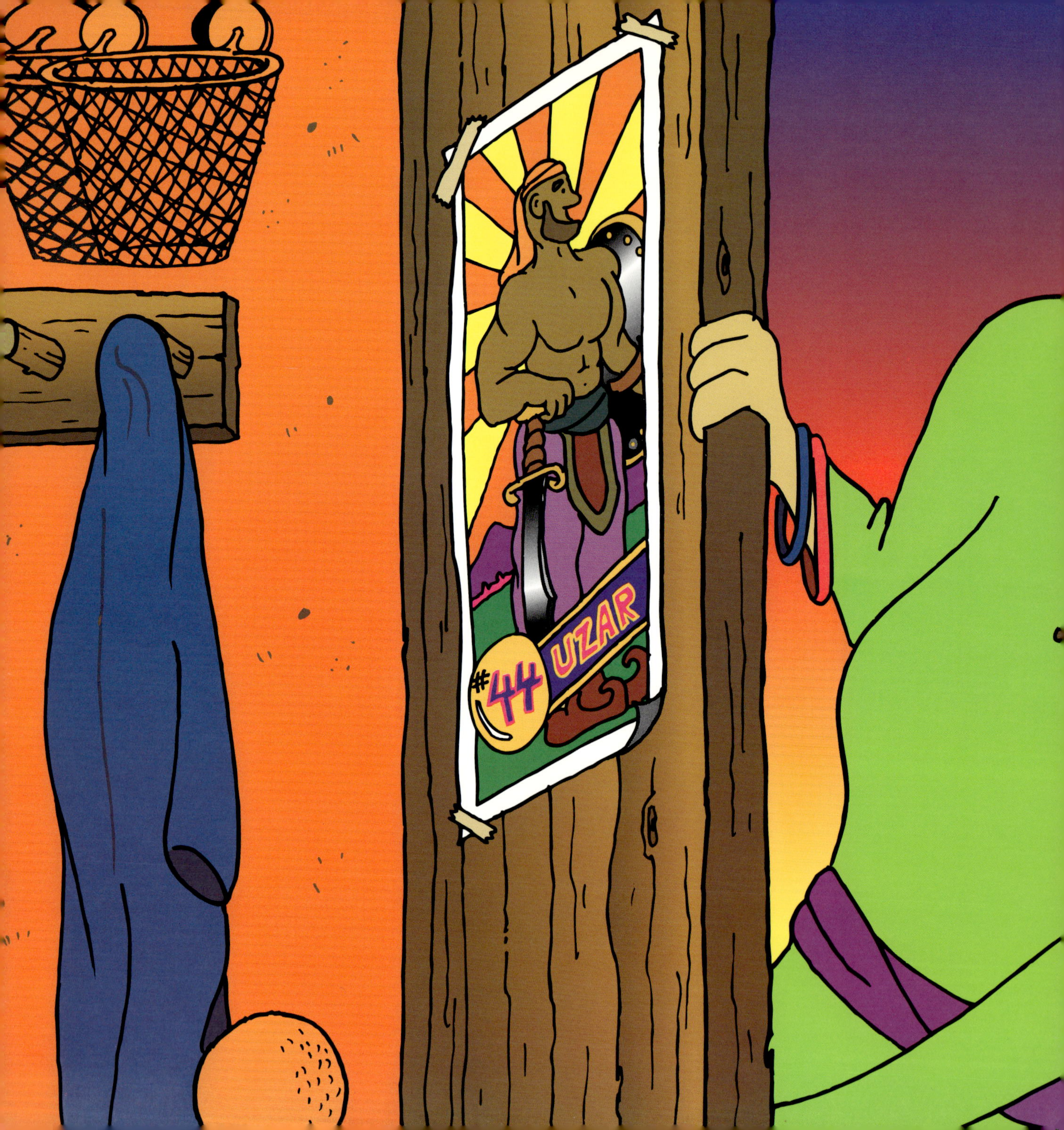
#44
UZAR

The next day the boy's mother woke him and told him that Jesus was down by the lake. This made the boy very happy.

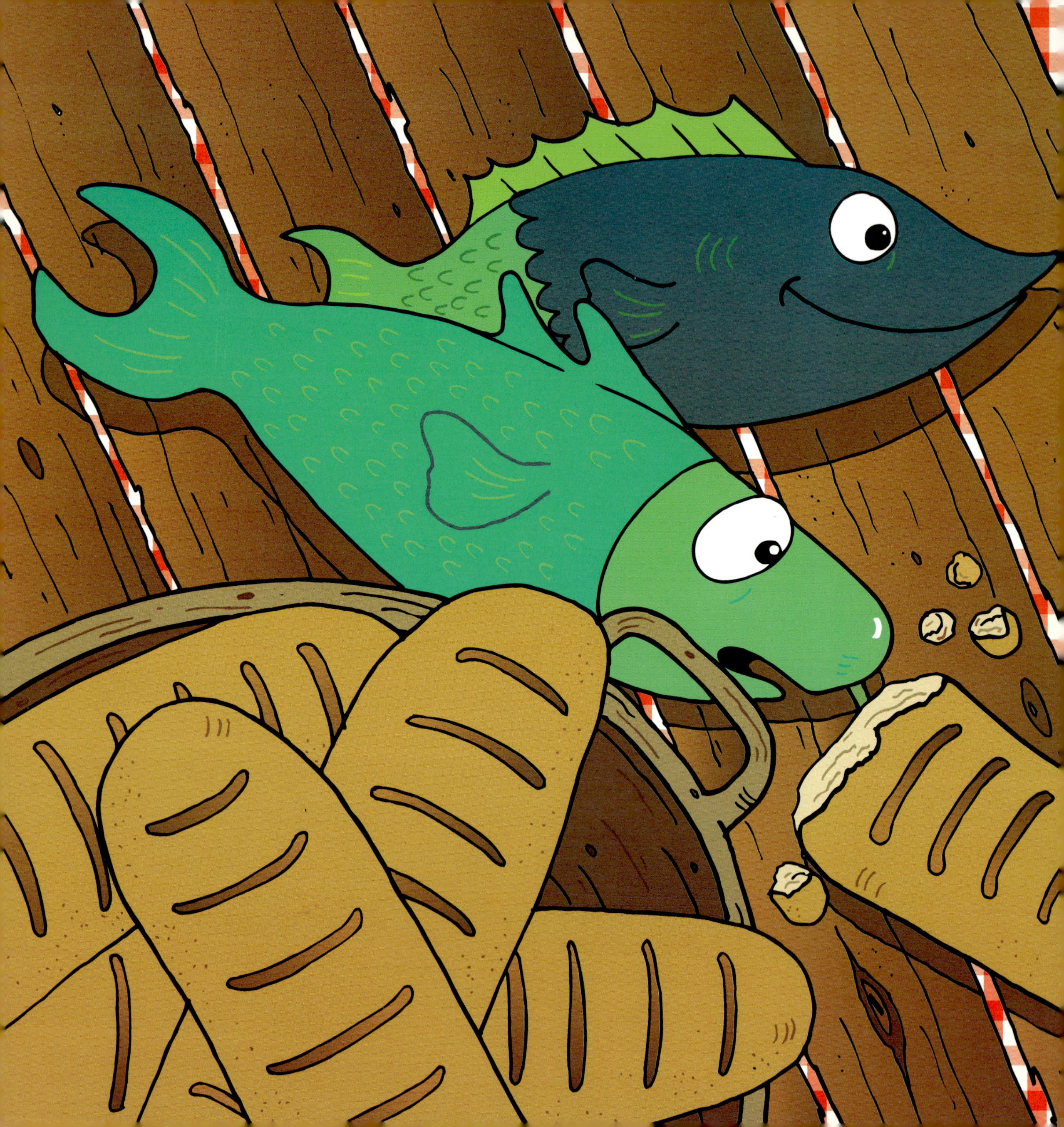

The boy hopped out of bed and grabbed five loaves of bread and two fish to eat later in the day. Then away he ran to see Jesus.

Finally the boy got close to Jesus and His disciples! Everywhere he looked, there were people--more people than he could count.

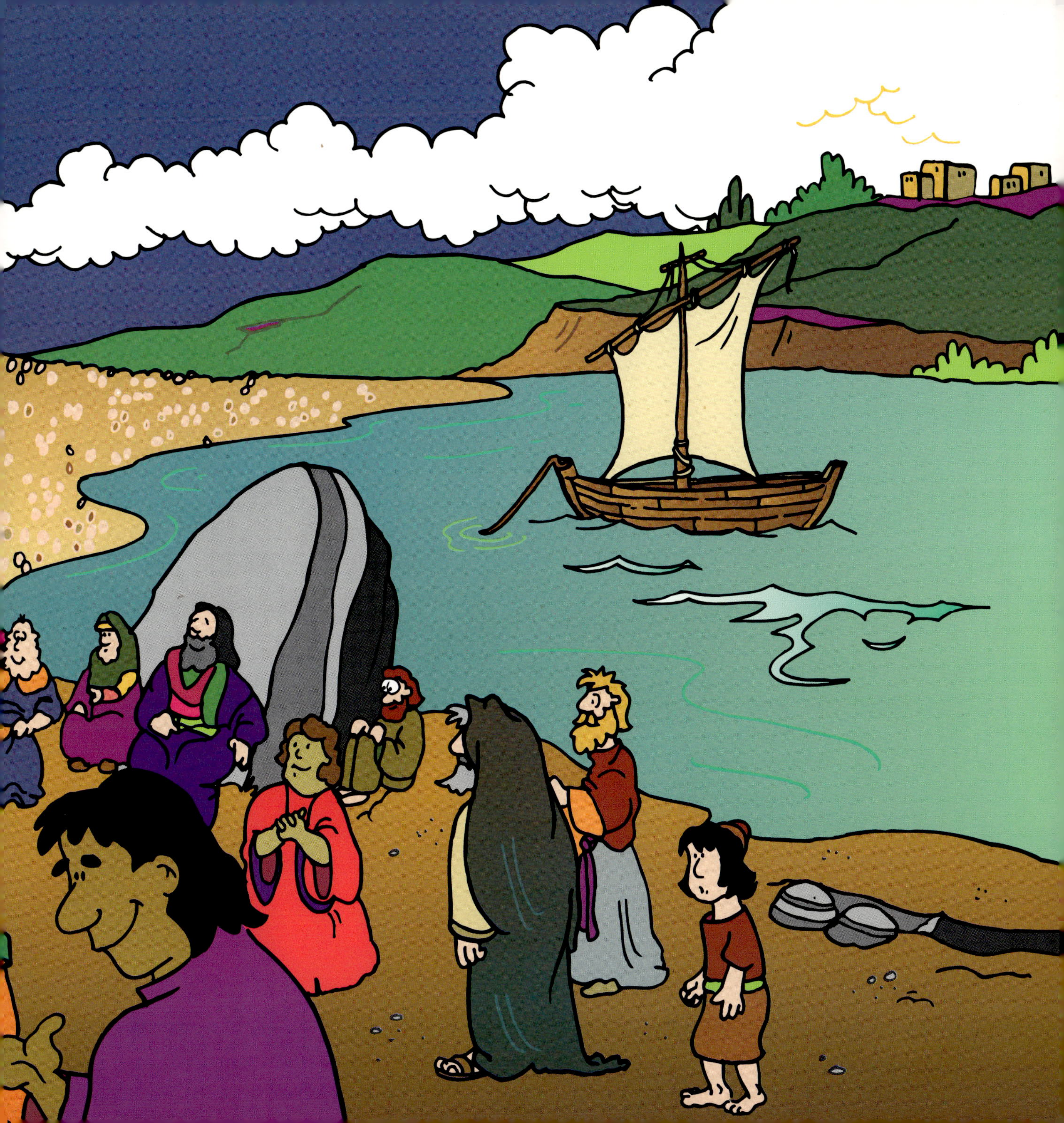

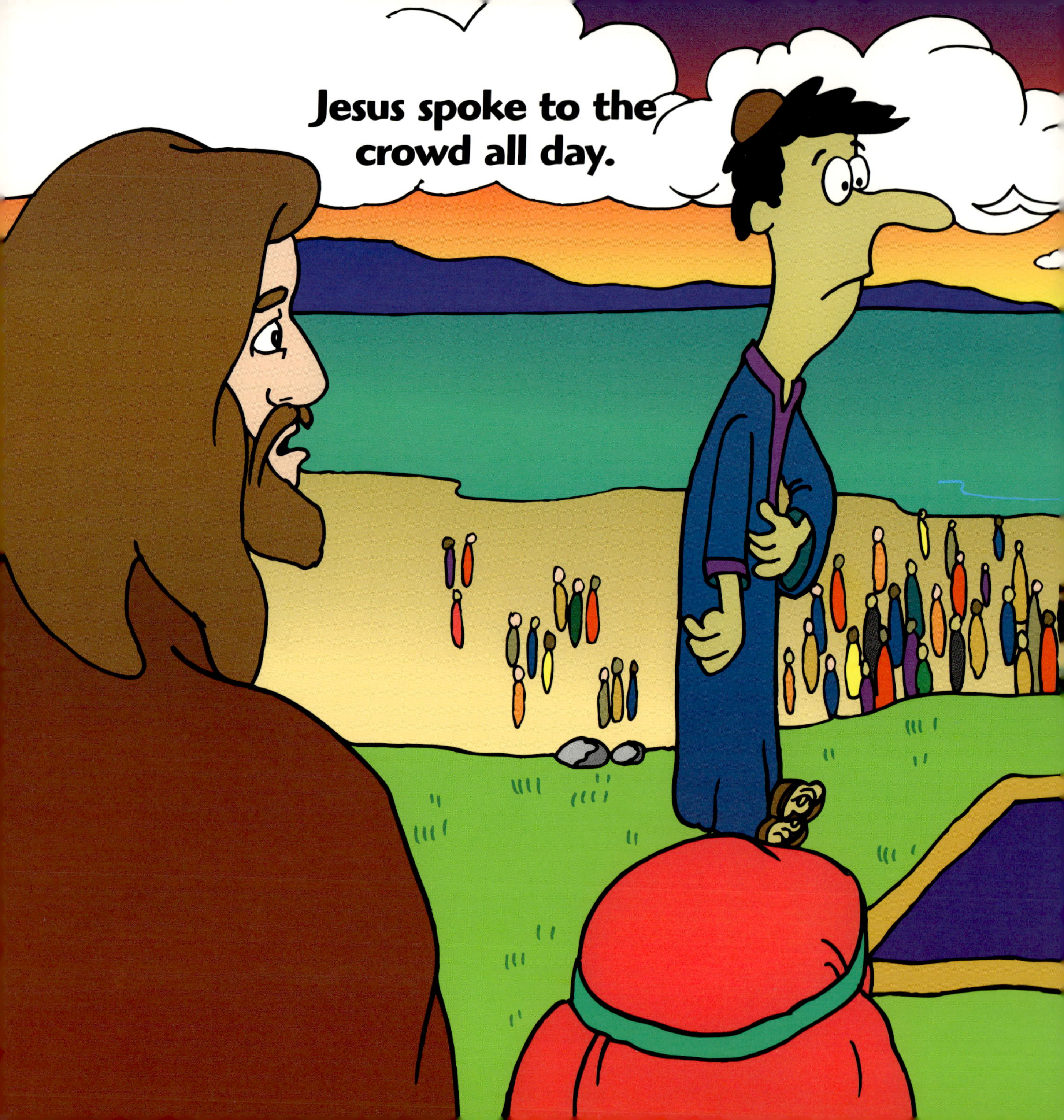
Jesus spoke to the
crowd all day.

At dinnertime Jesus saw that the people were really hungry.

The disciples asked Jesus if they should send everyone home to eat. Jesus told the disciples to feed all of the people.

But they answered, "How can we feed them? We don't have enough money to buy food."

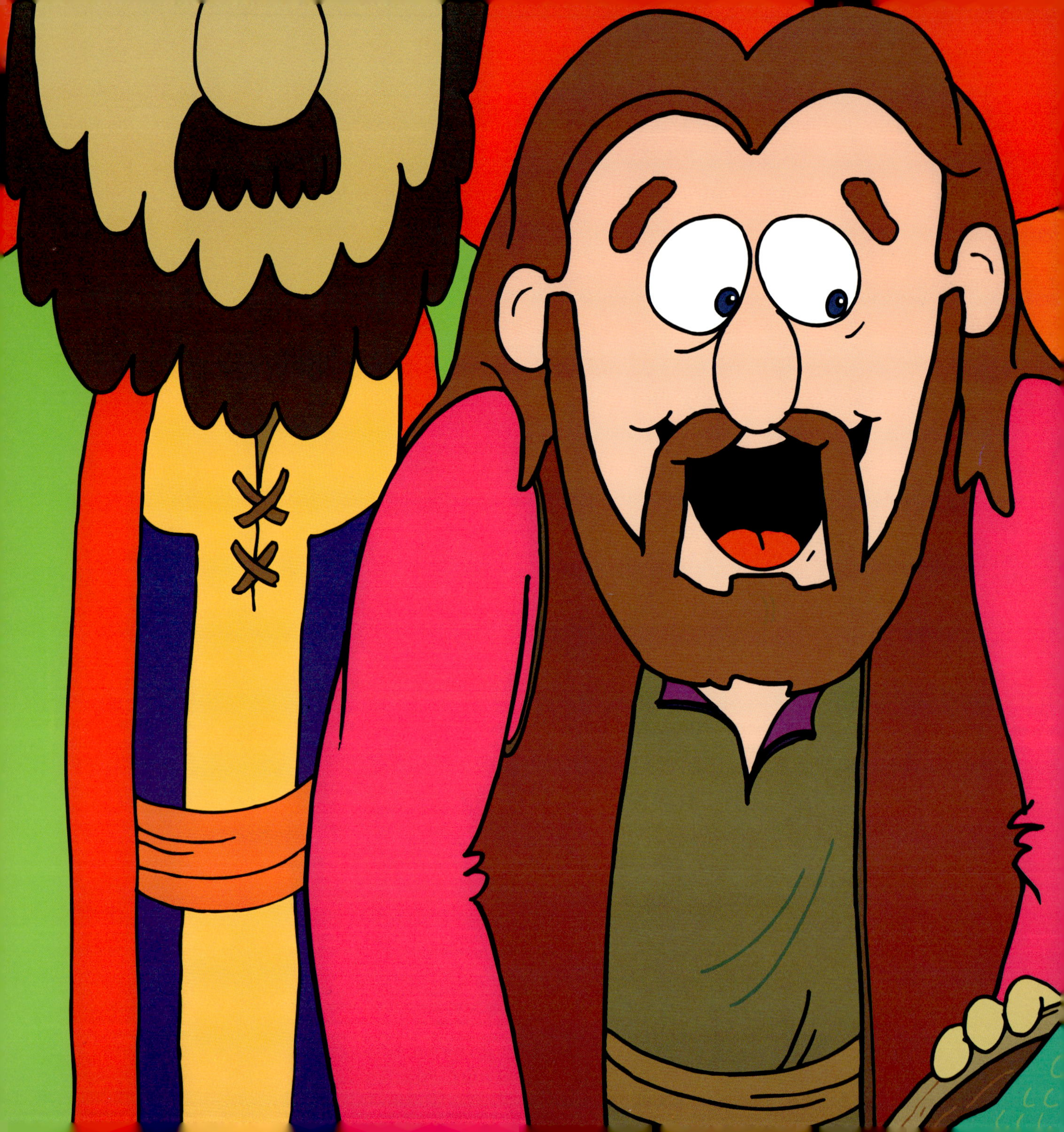

The disciples saw the boy and asked him to share his food. When he did, Jesus looked at him and smiled. Jesus was glad the boy had shared.

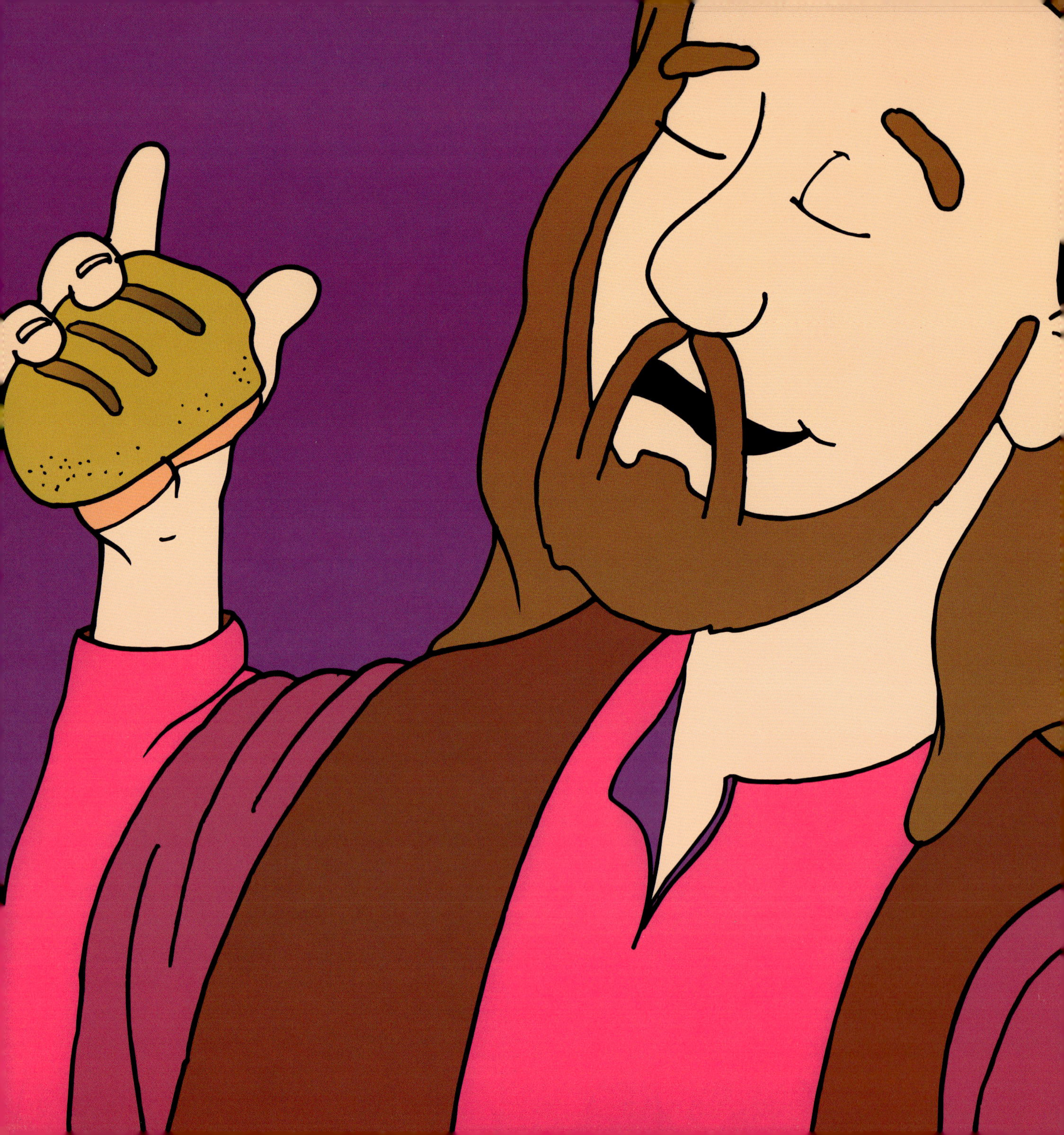

Jesus told everyone to sit on the soft grass. Then Jesus took the boy's bread and fish and thanked God for the food. He gave it to the disciples to feed the people.

Everyone ate until their tummies were full. Jesus told the disciples to pick up the leftover food so nothing would be wasted. They collected twelve big baskets of food.

The boy was very excited that Jesus had used his food to feed everyone. He couldn't wait to tell his family all Jesus had done.

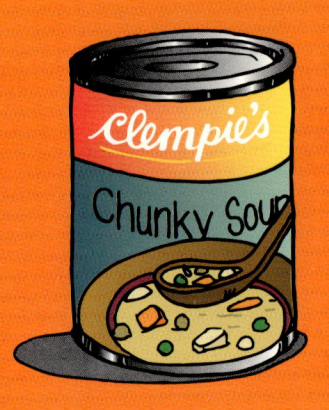

God can take even the littlest things
we have to share with others

and turn them into the biggest blessings.